Positive Thinking

Eradicate Pessimistic Thoughts Emotional Intelligence: A Self Help Book For Cultivating Mindfulness And Conquering Negative Thoughts

(Uncover The Influence Of Positive Thinking And Alter Your Mental Attitude To Transform Into An Optimist)

FaridMironova

TABLE OF CONTENT

Give And Take: How Putting Others' Needs First Will Cause Them To Put You First 1

Program Your Mind For The Best 5

Recognizing The Influence Of Positive Thoughts ... 18

Cognitive Behavioral Techniques: The Ultimate Weapons For Adverse Thoughts. 28

Thirty Small Habits Assist In Mentally Strong Development 43

The Mind As An Artist's Palette 54

How To Modify Your Attitude 74

How Is Eft Tapping Operational? 90

Make Use Of Your Strong Mind 103

Discover How To Identify The Correct Problem .. 112

Rewriting The Script: How To Rewire Your Thought Process 121

Bringing Your Inner Drive To Life 140

Putting Your Attention On Positivity 153

Give And Take: How Putting Others' Needs First Will Cause Them To Put You First

Getting attention is fundamental to our identity as human beings. Even though people are social beings who need company, many only consider their interests. Consequently, many believe that they are neither wanted nor required by others.

Thankfully, we can take certain actions to increase our likeability.

You have to first realize that the reason other people detest you stems from your mindset. Fortunately, you can change your mindset to fit in with others if you learn to become comfortable.

One prominent example of a happy person is James A. Farley, the former US Postmaster General. Practically everyone loved him since he had the right attitude. Some described him as "honest," "natural," and "comfortably outgoing."

Think about the people you like: Do they express interest in you, or do they only talk about themselves all the time? They probably say they're interested in you, and you should say the same. If you demonstrate to people that you are interested in their work, identity, and other facets of their lives, they will want to be kind to you in return.

For example, the author once assisted a patient at his clinic who thought everyone was against him. In the end, he realized that his excessive self-love and conceited mindset were the cause of this. After that, he established a list of everyone he met daily and made an effort to interact and get to know them as distinct individuals.

He quickly discovered love and gratitude by focusing on others and not on himself.

Certain people will be hard to like. However, if you work hard enough, you might uncover hidden benefits in even them.

Program Your Mind For The Best

You will hold the key to your life if you can train your thoughts. A great deal of our conceptions about how life functions are completely false. The majority of our views have never been put to the test in real life. Still, we operate under the assumption that our beliefs are accurate throughout our entire lives.

Through perception, humans have been collecting data about the nature of life over the years. Our issue is that our compiled data often represents our interpretation of the truth rather than the actual situation.

Our belief system constantly serves as a filter for what we see and hear. Our interpretation of reality is the story we tell ourselves about what we believe we hear or see. Our subconscious does not discriminate between what we are truly experiencing and imagining, even though we know the difference. The key takeaway is that, although we are aware of the differences, our subconscious minds only accept what our conscious minds acknowledge as true. It makes sense that we may alter our behavior using the same technique if this is the case and our opinions, beliefs, and expectations have been formed by vivid imagined experiences.

Beliefs: Viable and Viable Not

Every piece of knowledge we have been given is subconsciously preserved. That knowledge shapes our opinions and beliefs, influencing how we see ourselves. As far as we can tell, that is the truth, which shapes the prevailing perception of reality.

We must constantly assess our views to determine whether they are reasonable. In other words, do they help us achieve our goals and add to or detract from our sense of fulfillment and happiness?

If they don't work, we must rewire our subconscious to accept new beliefs. We must make the time to perform the required reprogramming. Since we are constantly being programmed, we have no control over whether or not we will be programmed. Who will conduct the programming is the decision that needs to be made. Will we perform the task ourselves or delegate it to someone else?

In all honesty, nobody else in the world cares about you the way you care about yourself. No matter how kind-hearted, you must refuse to let anyone conduct the programming for you.

The World's Most Potent Force

Whatever you think is true, your subconscious will make it happen. Since dawn, belief has been the fundamental component of all great accomplishments. We must constantly remind ourselves that our beliefs control our actions, making us the masters of our lives. However, we have the power to alter our beliefs, and the exciting part of this is that when we do so, we also alter our experiences, which are the product or outcome of our beliefs. It is always up to us to decide what we want to believe. We never have to stay stuck with outdated, unproductive ideas forever.

One may legitimately argue that belief is the most potent force in existence. Helen Keller overcame great challenges despite being blind and deaf because of her beliefs. Belief is a power that can either assist or destroy us. It kept Einstein going until he found the theory of relativity, but it also gave people the ability to commit suicide, start wars, and live lives of crime. Reprogramming ourselves and creating an atmosphere where our beliefs help us achieve our goals is what we want to do. Positive self-talk phrases and images are the instruments we employ to achieve this.

Reaffirmations and Picture

Simply said, positive self-talk aims to mentally surround oneself with beliefs reinforcing a particular behavior or experience. Positive self-talk claims frequently don't reflect the situation's reality as it stands now. They are predicated on our desired state of affairs.

Imaging, or visualization, describes the mind's capacity to create mental images of objects. It is essentially a concept that we focus on for long enough to form an aware mental and emotional image. Another name for visualization is "applied imagination." It is among our most important tools for bringing about change.

As we already discovered, our beliefs about our thoughts give rise to reality. Every day, we have thousands of thoughts, but the ones that are emotionally charged are those that impact us. Visualization is taking a concept and holding onto it long enough for our mental image to elicit an emotional reaction. Remember that conviction comes from thought plus emotion, and reality comes from conviction.

Affirmations are high-quality concepts and ideas. Our lives are reflected in the caliber of our thinking. Therefore, we would inevitably live better lives if we were to elevate the caliber of our thinking.

The effectiveness of positive imagery and positive self-talk For You

Autosuggestions generate profound Self-Talk phrases. Emile Coue employed autosuggestion with great success in his French clinic around the turn of the century. He instructed his patients to say to themselves, "Every day, I am getting better and better in every way." Positive self-talk operates on displacement, which worked because of the consistent repetition. When you place a glass of unclean water under the faucet and run clean water into it, the dirty water will gradually be replaced by clean water. The same happens when you swap out negative, unproductive thoughts for constructive, productive ones. Eliminating limiting thoughts that we have within our subconscious is not a must. Making sure that our prevailing beliefs help us achieve our goals rather than hinder us.

GIGO is a term used in computer language. Pronounce that like a "ge-go." "Garbage in - garbage out" is what it stands for. Essentially, it indicates that you should anticipate getting the incorrect response if you ask a computer a question after giving it all the incorrect data. What is a computer's weakest point right now? Of course, the weakest link is the computer programmer.

The programmer's input will be inaccurate if their view of reality is flawed. This implies that when the computer is asked to solve a problem, it will provide inaccurate feedback since the data it receives is inaccurate. Similarly, if the wrong data—illogical or inaccurate—is fed to your conscious mind—your programmer—the translation will also be flawed.

Contradictory ideas cannot coexist. This implies that you are unable to hold two contradictory ideas at once. Since you cannot think "I can" and "I can't" about the same item simultaneously, it is critical to recognize and rewire your prevailing thought patterns. It's true what Emerson stated when he said, "We become what we think about all day long." Walking and verbal proof of our convictions is what you and I both do.

As we've covered, one of the best strategies for programming your subconscious to think positively is to use positive self-talk. Another name for positive self-talk is affirmation. Since the word affirmation means to validate or confirm, we validate or confirm a concept as true when we consider it repeatedly. We are strengthening our conviction by creating a recording in our brain's neuronal structure, which is then processed by our subconscious mind. Once our subconscious embraces a belief, it is a concept whose time has come.

A daily affirmation practice is one of the simplest things we can do to make positive changes in our lives. The majority of individuals are not familiar with proper affirmation usage. All you need to know for now is that imprinting your affirmations is simple; you will discover an easy approach in Chapter 7.

We must use imagery with affirmations and self-talk to get the best outcomes. One may argue that every idea we have is a mental image. You immediately see a dog when I mention dogs. When I use an abstract word like bravery, I have to think about it until I can distill the meaning to a mental image of courage.

You have likely said to someone, "I'm not able to get the picture," at some point. You cannot grasp the picture if you are confused and unable to comprehend what someone is attempting to tell you. The act of retaining an idea in your mind until it materializes as an image or mental picture is known as imagery or visualization. The mental image or picture lets you experience it and feel there. We call this applied imagination. The distinction between imagery and affirmations is that the former are deliberate thoughts you choose to entertain. More is done with imagery. It takes those ideas and meditates on them until feelings and convictions are produced.

Daydreaming is not the same as imagery or visualization. Using predefined attitudes and beliefs to attain a specific objective, imagery is a deliberate procedure. Building the confidence needed to act is the goal of visualizing.

Daydreams are not planned conscious thoughts that reinforce attitudes or beliefs but diverge from reality. The human brain and nerve system collaborate to create a sensory response mechanism that automatically responds to obstacles and issues, which is why imagery is effective. Visualization captures recollections and shapes attitudes and ideas even before the event occurs. It enables us to store the information we want as our interpretation of reality in our subconscious minds.

Never forget that our perception of reality is our own. This is made possible by the inability of our subconscious mind to discern between vividly imagined and real experiences. Our subconscious absorbs anything we vividly and intensely conceive through the direction of images as though it were real. Everything we go through when our subconscious accepts what we imagine is connected to the newly created belief or image.

Succeeding requires affirmation, imagery, and emotion.

To create effective imagery, try to convey as much emotion as possible. Excite yourself, arouse a strong inner desire, and run the image repeatedly. Because thought and feeling combined create your current beliefs, if you invest enough emotion in your new ideas, they will overpower the old ones and eliminate them from your mind. Repetition trains new ideas, and imagery takes over as the main idea. Our prevailing thoughts and beliefs dictate our behavior. We've all shown that this is effective.

When you worry about something, you mentally create a clear picture of the worst-case scenario. You listen to it repeatedly. All you are doing is talking about and visualizing the outcome; you are not exerting effort or willpower. Even though what you are imagining hasn't happened yet, you can't stop drawing and seeing it. The image gets increasingly real since you've come to terms with the possibility of a bad ending; you've been thinking about it as truth and replaying the image all the time. After a while, you start to automatically produce the feelings that fit the picture; you start to feel tension, dread, anxiety, discouragement, and depression. A fictitious experience caused this whole mess!

It's important to emphasize that worrying has no recognized benefits and cannot alter the course of events; however, it can erode your faith, impair your judgment, sabotage your inner peace of mind, and leave you feeling helpless.

Recognizing TheInfluence Of Positive Thoughts

Have you ever thought about how your brain shapes your daily reality? It can create beauty out of nothing and has amazing potential. Feeling excited instead of nervous would be a huge difference since optimistic feelings inspire courage and hope, which are beneficial in trying circumstances. Have faith that it will lead to something wonderful; if you're tenacious, you'll get there!

What precisely is positive thinking, though? In essence, it indicates that regardless of what is happening around us, we should focus on the positive rather than lingering too long on the negative. Concentrating on the positives can maintain optimism and self-assurance during difficult times. Just picture the sunny side of the sky anytime a storm is approaching! These encouraging ideas can help us remember our aims while encountering difficulties, which motivates us to keep moving forward and accomplish our objectives even when we encounter obstacles.

You may be wondering if people can control their destinies or if optimism affects how life unfolds. The good news is that research points to a yes (Boas, 2022). Adopting a positive outlook empowers individuals to take an active role in shaping their destiny rather than merely responding to events beyond their control. Everyone has the opportunity to better mold who they are! You must practice positive self-talk frequently, acting as though you've already achieved your goals despite your current difficulties. Then, the concept steadily advances us.

Positive thinking affects all facets of life, including friendships, performance at work, and physical health, and goes beyond simply making you feel good right now. Additionally, concentrating on positivity starts a domino effect that makes everything else fall into place. You become more resilient, capable of handling adversity, and open to new opportunities.

This anecdote illustrates how perspective impacts happiness: Despite making $150 an hour, the man was not content. No matter how much money he had, he never felt satisfied compared to others who appeared wealthy. His poor thoughts about his wage, compared to his contemporaries who made more money, cast a shadow over his enjoyment, even though he received a magnificent paycheck.

There was another resident in that same town, but he had little wealth or material possessions to show for it. People would characterize him as content and calm despite this deficiency, though, since he expressed thanks and had a positive outlook on life while making only $50 a day—a pittance compared to others.

They discussed and placed orders for their favorite drinks at the café where they first met. The unhappy individual thought the joyful person had something unique and was curious to know more. He talked about how having nice things didn't make him feel empty and asked if the joyful person had any tricks for achieving inner contentment. Over warm drinks, they talked about such questions and then moved on to other topics.

In a gracious reply, the contented man said, "I'm grateful for what I have since I can provide for my loved ones." That makes me feel good about myself," the unhappy man said, and it had such a profound effect on him that he couldn't stop asking questions to get insight from such sage advice!

As the conversation continued, the angry man realized he didn't value his current belongings enough, and perhaps he should learn to be content rather than constantly wishing for bigger and greater things in the future. After discussing various subjects for a few hours until the café closed, they went outside.

Life lesson learned: Don't judge yourself by the standards of others; prosperity and well-being are not the same! Thus, give greater gratitude for what brings you joy now and in the future, as this ultimately matters most. Find methods to help others so that, even in the darkest times, you can survive. Riches do not equate to health either, and isolation has negative effects, so be open, share with people, and try to connect once.

Dismantling Obstacles: Dissecting Adverse Thoughts

I picture you getting ready for a big day while standing in front of a mirror. However, the voice in your reflection whispering, "You're just not good enough for this," is a critic rather than a supporter. Does that sound familiar? That's your inner critic, a master of disguise who frequently goes by the guise of a "reality check" and "realism." The catch is that these notions are just perceptions, and perceptions are malleable. They are not the infallible truth. As my therapist would say, "Emotions aren't facts!" It is accurate. Emotions and how you see yourself have great power. They are an attempt by your mind to shield you from harm and disappointment. You are ultimately in charge of your thoughts, though.

Our minds are amazing; they can be our strongest ally or our deadliest enemy. Negative thoughts frequently result from feelings of inadequacy or self-doubt. Consider for a second when you were doubting yourself. Perhaps it was the belief that you were too dim to contribute to a group debate. That's the voice of your inner critic. The first step to better managing our emotions is to recognize our thoughts for what they are: thoughts, not facts, as noted psychologist Dr. Susan David advises.

Identifying Patterns of Negative Thought: Recognizing Intruders: Awareness is the first step to transformation. It's critical to identify these harmful mental processes. You can discover that you're mired in a cycle of negative thinking, such as "I'll never succeed." This is a widespread negative thought habit. Other typical tendencies include personalizing—taking things too personally—and catastrophizing—

blowing things out of proportion. Psychology Today states that recognizing these tendencies is essential to comprehending and testing our mental processes. How these thoughts make you feel is a fantastic way to identify them. When you mentally depress yourself, do you have a knot in your stomach? That's a pessimistic idea.

Cognitive Behavioral Techniques: The Ultimate Weapons For Adverse Thoughts.

Now, enter Cognitive Behavioral Therapy (C.B.T.C.B.T.), a formidable tool for overcoming negative thought patterns. Imagine that you are criticizing and calling yourself a failure for not completing a project by the deadline. C.B.T.C.B.T. helps us to question these ideas. Seek proof that the opposite is true, such as your prior achievements. Think about if you're looking at the situation from every perspective. Were there outside forces at play? Research from the Mayo Clinic demonstrates that C.B.T.C.B.T. techniques can dramatically improve optimism and reduce depressive symptoms. My therapist specializes in cognitive behavioral therapy (C.B.T.C.B.T.).

The domain of ideas and self-awareness is your Sherlock Holmes. It's identifying that depressing sensation after looking through Facebook and understanding that it results from comparison. When I would compare myself to other high school females, my mother always said, "Comparison is the thief of joy!" We often find ourselves thinking about other people's lives and contrasting them with our own. Self-awareness involves realizing the connection between negative self-talk and actions such as staying away from social gatherings. According to the

American Psychological Association, better emotional regulation and a more optimistic outlook are directly correlated with increased self-awareness.

Real-Life Metamorphosis: Changing the Adverse into the Positive

The great aspect is that all it takes to turn these negatives into positives is a simple revision of your self-talk. Try stating something like, "Balancing parenting and work is challenging, but I'm giving it my best," as opposed to, "I can't handle my kids and my job." Positive self-talk and thought change significantly improve happiness and quality of life.

We have started to break down the walls of pessimistic thinking in this chapter. We've begun to comprehend, identify, and confront these ideas. It's time to eliminate the old, worn-out pessimism to make room for new, upbeat ideas, much like when you organize your closet. Recall that the first step towards living a happy life is comprehending and changing our thinking. As the saying goes, "Your reality is what you perceive."

Section Five

Increasing Survival

In this chapter, Frankie presents the idea of increasing life or the notion that everything in the universe is constantly developing and expanding.

He contends that to become wealthy; one must adhere to this idea and work to improve both their own and other people's quality of life.

The Increasing Life Principle

He introduces the idea of increasing life at the outset. He contends that everything in the cosmos is always growing and expanding and that adhering to this idea will help one become wealthy: "The principle of increasing life is the foundation of all success and abundance." It is the notion that everything in the cosmos is ever-expanding and growing and that we should all strive to prolong both our own and other people's lives."

He says that one can start drawing prosperity and success into one's life by concentrating on growth and expansion instead of contraction and limitation.

The Value of Assistance

The significance of service in aligning oneself with the notion of enhancing life is then covered by Frankie. He contends that one must put others' needs and contributions to the world above their own to become wealthy: We improve our lives and generate wealth and prosperity for ourselves and others around us by attempting to add value and serve others."

He says that one can connect oneself with the idea of enhancing life and attracting abundance and success into one's life by concentrating on offering value and service and by attempting to have a positive impact on the world.

The Compensation Law

He explains the law of compensation, which holds that a person's benefits in life are closely correlated with the value they offer others. He contends that to become wealthy, one must concentrate on adding more value than they are paid for: "According to the law of compensation, we are compensated in life according to the value we add to the lives of others. We accord with the idea of increasing life and draw abundance into our lives when we strive to provide more worth than we are compensated for."

He says that one can start drawing more money and benefits into one's life by concentrating on offering value and service and continuously working to raise the value one offers.

Creative vs. Competitive Thinking

He then makes a distinction between thinking processes that are competitive and creative. He claims: "Competitive thought patterns are rooted in fear and scarcity, and ultimately lead to limitation and lack." He claims that a competitive mentality, which emphasizes taking from others and competing for limited resources, is ultimately restricting and counterproductive. Conversely, creative thought patterns centered on adding value and improving the environment align with the maxim "Increasing life leads to abundance and prosperity."

He encourages readers to let go of constricting ideas about scarcity and rivalry to concentrate on adding value and making a constructive contribution to the world.

In this chapter, Franklin presents the idea of rising life or the notion that everything in the cosmos is expanding and growing. He contends that to become wealthy; one must adhere to this idea and work to improve both their own and other people's quality of life. Highlights the significance of service and the idea that one can align oneself with the principle of growing life and draw prosperity and wealth into one's life by concentrating on adding worth to the world. Additionally, he presents the law of compensation, which holds that a person's gains are closely correlated with the value they offer others. Lastly, he distinguishes between the thought patterns that are competitive and creative, making the case that one can create a more abundant and prosperous reality by letting go of limiting beliefs about competition and scarcity and concentrating instead on adding value and positively impacting the world.

The Summary of +Points

"Being aware is the first step toward transformation. Acceptance is the second stage." 1.

We've reviewed the conventional approaches to fostering optimism and each one's lack of sustained effectiveness. We've examined the inner workings of negativity, that naughty little monster, and how it affects our playdough ball. Additionally, to ensure that the solutions we implement are effective, we have examined evidence-based foundations. Let's now dissect the key ideas in the .framework to understand The +Point Process. Yes, don't they all enjoy a good acronym?

The Building Blocks of the +Point Process

The R.E.S.E.T.R.E.S.E.T. Framework is the essential component of The +Point Process's framework. When combined with a fantastic transformation plan, these building blocks will take you step-by-step through the stages of awareness, acceptance, adoption, and advocacy. Think of them as breakfast, lunch, and dinner, with a delicious little dessert.

Let's take a closer look at the framework and familiarize ourselves with its five main tenets, which will be useful later in our adventure.

First Principle: Acknowledge

This is where your adventure begins. Acknowledgment is the first step in everything. It's similar to venturing into the unknown area only to have Google Maps thrust before you. Understanding your surroundings is as important as studying the lay of the land before embarking on a new journey. We're talking about identifying the mental landscape in this fundamental process step—those thought patterns that seize your hand and take you in either a positive or bad direction.

Second Principle: Investigate

So here we are, exploring the territory of self-awareness like contemporary explorers. This is where we dig deep into our psyche's inner workings and roll up our sleeves. Imagine it like putting on a miner's helmet and exploring the various tunnels and caverns within your mind. Here, you'll find hidden gems: the convictions, life lessons, and intricate mental processes you let dictate your response to particular circumstances. It's similar to going on a mental odyssey and discovering untapped potential while negotiating the maze of your ideas.

Third Principle: Adjust

We are currently winning the war against negativity and are on the rise. One of the key components of The +Point Process is changing from a negative to a positive mindset. It's important to alter your viewpoint of problems as they appear rather than denying their presence. It's similar to getting the ideal pair of glasses or fine-tuning your lens so you can see the opportunities despite all the obstacles. Once you get the hang of it, you'll discover that you're taking a fresh tack and navigating the difficult patches of life with a resurgence of energy, tenacity, and achievement.

Thirty Small Habits Assist In Mentally Strong Development

Everyone wants to get off to a great start in the new year, but finishing strong is just as vital. A lot of resolutions and objectives never get accomplished because we become mired in our daily lives and lack the mental fortitude to persevere once the excitement of the festivities wanes.

But achieving your objectives and going above and beyond them often comes down to having a strong mental toughness reserve for those trying times. When discipline is created, it will support your ongoing capacity to make wise decisions that will lead to your goals. Remind yourself not to give up what you truly desire for the moment's pleasure.

Gaining mental strength doesn't have to be difficult; here are some helpful hints and techniques. In the same way, physical strength requires exercise to maintain strong muscles; mental strength requires exercise to support the development of habits and beliefs.

Finding routines and quick fixes throughout the day to maintain a positive outlook and high energy and developing skills and habits that will help you go forward and feel good about what you're doing is one of the finest methods to strengthen your mental fortitude. In the interim, you're strengthening your mental fortitude in a method that won't wear you out or overwhelm you.

Apply some of these suggestions to become a happier and more resilient person mentally:

1. The condition of your mattress. Making your bed first thing in the morning means you're already progressing and off to a terrific start. "The condition of your bed is the state of your head" is a proverb you may recall. It has a lot of truth to it. It may seem like a little step, but there are a lot of advantages.

Studies reveal that persons who make their beds daily are generally happier, more productive, and feel more pleasure and success in completing all the chores in their day. This small action establishes the habit of doing tasks first thing in the morning.

2. Reduce your negative self-talk every day. Decide to speak to yourself more positively and to reduce the amount of negative self-talk. When you become the biggest fan in your mind, you can initially feel stupid, but picture how wonderful it will feel to make greater choices in your life. It's those same choices that will propel you forward toward your objective.

Be alert; negative ideas can infiltrate rapidly. Once you identify a negative thought, simply label it false and replace it with a good one.

3. Foster appreciation. Write something wonderful daily, and save it anywhere you like—in a jar, a journal, a shoe box, etc. This cultivates thankfulness in your life.

Take a seat and reflect on the good things you've gone through and achieved rather than just the difficulties or difficult times that ultimately made you want to give up.

4. Modify your viewpoint. Perspective plays a big part in life. You can alter your life by altering your point of view.

By outlining the positive parts of the problems and the lessons you could gain from them, you can strengthen your mental strength and avoid getting upset, angry, or disappointed about any challenges that may arise. Make an effort to be thankful for something each day.

5. When traveling, cultivate conscious happiness. Being mindful involves living in the present. Practice being deliberately joyful until you feel comfortable being happy.

Choose a time, place, or memory when you're feeling happy and allow yourself to fully experience that emotion. Take note of how it feels, how your body feels, how your thoughts shift, and whether it seems to be associated with any particular color.

Go for a while in your joyful state of mind. Finally, take note of your feelings of joy and happiness. These are yours and arise naturally when you are present and aware of the present moment.

6. Make it a regular habit to be your best buddy. This is a fantastic method to develop mental toughness since it teaches us to rely on ourselves and not depend on others to help us get up.

The next time, something doesn't happen exactly as expected. If you find yourself insulting or criticizing yourself, stop and consider if you would allow your best friend to treat you or yourself similarly.

It's a good idea to love yourself just as much as, if not more, than your best buddy because the likelihood is that the answer is no.

7. Get adept at saying "No" without justification. Somewhere along the road, society decided that refusing something only has to have a valid cause; simply wanting to do something isn't enough. Throw that way of thinking out if you find yourself thinking that way.

Acquire the ability to refuse. You are under no need to defend your choices or explain why you are not willing to do something.

8. Every day, dedicate ten minutes to self-care. No matter who you are or what you do, you will eventually run out of resources and be unable to love and

care for people around you if you don't take the time to truly care for yourself.

Self-care can be as elaborate as getting a manicure or treating yourself to a spa day, or it can be as straightforward as spending ten minutes alone in a room to decompress. Allow Tony Robbins' statement to sink in if you believe you don't have ten minutes: "If you don't have ten minutes, you don't have a life." Whatever it is, set aside time and/or engage in activities that satisfy and uplift you.

9. Give up a habit that makes you happy. This is a beneficial self-care method. Try to find something to do or a pastime you enjoy merely to boost your mood.

As you get better at it and gain confidence in your abilities, you'll find that these feelings of self-worth will seep into other aspects of your life. You'll become mentally stronger when you take on the more difficult components of your chosen objective, thanks to your positive self-talk and enjoyment of your activity.

10. Make it your mission to be more appreciative and less whiny. Not only can whining become a habit that makes you difficult to be around, but Try to find something for which to be thankful rather than just venting your frustrations all the time.

11. Getting at least eight hours of sleep every night. When they are very

exhausted, you have witnessed little children go crazy. Adults are the same way, albeit we rarely pass out during a meal. Overtiredness causes you to make bad decisions, lose mental clarity, think like a six-year-old, and cause your body to release more stress hormones.

Prioritize getting enough sleep to maintain your mental toughness. If you're an athlete of any kind, you should get at least eight hours; the more, the better. If you're under stress, give yourself enough time to unwind and rest before bed so your body can get the most out of your sleep.

The Mind As An Artist's Palette

The Perceptual Power

We investigate the depths of the human mind by looking at perception. This is where the canvas of our reality is initially prepped and stretched. Our perception serves as a lens through which we view the world, greatly influencing our thoughts, feelings, and behaviors.

The fine art of perceiving the world via the prism of our perspective is called perception. It serves as the prism through which we view the symphony of life, transforming the commonplace into the exceptional and the remarkable into the banal. The ability to perceive is a gift that encourages us to discover life's wonders.

Think of the world as a gallery where every second is a work of art waiting to be appreciated. The lens of human perception intensifies colors, deepens emotions, and gives experiences greater significance. The secret to revealing the extraordinary concealed within the ordinary is right here in this lens.

The compass that directs us on our trip is the power of perception. It turns obstacles into stepping stones and failures into learning experiences. It demonstrates the value of obstacles, the beauty in flaws, and the bright side of hardship. It is the catalyst for our imagination, the force behind our aspirations, and the creator of our world.

Our ability to perceive the world not just as it is but also as it could be is a wonderful gift. We can create our dreams, mold our realities, and bring the extraordinary to life in every instant we perceive.

The Perception Filters

Instead of being a clear window into reality, perception is a multifaceted process shaped by our emotions, experiences, and beliefs. These filters shape the way we perceive and comprehend the world around us. It all starts with how we see things, whether we see a glass as half full or half empty, a struggle as an opportunity or a setback, etc.

Because perception is flexible, it has the power to both constrain and liberate. The first step to comprehending how filters affect our perception is realizing what filters they impose on our thoughts. Do we have a positive perspective on the world, or is negativity obscuring our vision? Understanding these filters is essential to redefining our world.

Beliefs' Function

Our beliefs greatly influence our perception. These are the tenets of conduct that we have, frequently unknowingly, evolved over our lives. Our experiences can be painted on a canvas that is either larger or smaller by our beliefs about the world, ourselves, and our capacity.

Our perspective will be distorted if we have to limit ideas, such as the notion that we are unworthy, that success belongs to others, or that the world is unfriendly. Conversely, empowering beliefs can extend our outlook and create new opportunities.

Modifying Our Understanding

The fact that perception is malleable is excellent news. We can change how we perceive things by questioning and modifying our beliefs. We can change how we see the world by deliberately considering and modifying our beliefs. Through this process, we can adopt a growth- and resilience-oriented mentality and recognize opportunities where there were previously barriers.

What advantages can optimistic thinking offer?

More and more medical professionals now acknowledge the direct benefits of positive thinking and building a personal empowerment system (PES) for physical health. This is confirmed by so much research that it can no longer be disputed. Less is known about the numerous hypotheses explaining why positive thinking improves our health and lengthens our lives.

Stress is our response to circumstances that we consider to be dangerous. Stress is not inherently dangerous. It briefly activates our "fight or flight" reaction, assisting us in escaping the danger. When stress is constant, it becomes an issue. We refer to this as "chronic stress." Many people in the modern world have to juggle competing demands on their time and attention. There never seems to be enough time to complete everything well, and we feel we are tugged in multiple directions. Numerous direct bodily repercussions are associated with chronic stress. These consist of, but are not restricted to:

    elevated blood pressure
    pounding heart

A speeding heart and elevated blood pressure over time can raise the risk of a heart attack.

Breathing difficulties

compromise the immune system.

Decreased desire for sex

tense muscles that cause headaches, shoulder and back pain

Long-term stress is also closely linked to mental health problems. Problematic habits like binge eating, undereating, drug misuse, inactivity, and alcoholism might result from it. Insomnia and mood problems, including anxiety, anger, and even melancholy, can be brought on by it.

Many of us become so accustomed to dealing with stress daily that we stop noticing it. However, persistent stress impairs your health and happiness and will almost surely shorten your life expectancy.

You could eliminate stress by making radical life changes to avoid the factors that lead to it. You may go to the country, quit your work, and end your relationships. That isn't an option for most individuals, as it necessitates a significant adjustment to your professional and personal life. Remembering stress is not an inevitable aspect of leading a busy and successful life is critical. The environment around you does not cause stress. It all depends on how you view and respond to that world.

Your life's stressors won't go away just because you think positively. But it will alter your interpretation of those events, lessening the negative impacts of stress and all the emotional and physical issues it raises. The advantages of learning positive thinking strategies extend beyond that. This alone makes them worthwhile.

Personal and professional connections will benefit from adopting a more optimistic outlook. Consider the individuals you like to hang out with if that seems improbable. How many of those people are naysayers who constantly seem to be depressed and unhappy? How many are optimistic, confident, and upbeat? Most individuals would much rather be with someone who is always positive.

Positive thinkers also have higher success rates. Numerous studies have shown that optimistic people not only have more fulfilling relationships and successful occupations, but they also earn more money. Numerous research studies demonstrate happy people, money, work performance, and health, according to a meta-analysis of studies involving more than 275,000[5] people. The relationship between happiness and success is not just based on the fact that success leads to happiness; it also stems from positive affect.

In a different study, optimistic salespeople in the insurance industry made, on average, 88% more than their pessimistic counterparts.

Being positive involves more than just having an optimistic outlook on the future. It's an attitude toward life that will improve your financial situation, well-being, and health. This book teaches you to adopt an optimistic outlook on life, enabling you to reap all those substantial advantages.

To whom does the whole content pertain?

The entire text is meant for anyone who wants to alter their life but is unsure of how to go about it or who wants to change but doesn't know how.

Once you've perused every chapter, you'll understand how to improve your life. No matter how old or committed you are, there's always a good time to wake up from slumber. Everyday life gives us the harsh taste of our choices but also showers us with the sweetness of little triumphs. Should the majority of your choices mislead you? However, when everything appears to be running smoothly, we might not investigate if there might be a more sinister cause. Most individuals generally move forward blindly, taking life as it comes; sometimes, things work out, and sometimes they don't. Sometimes, it feels like life is one giant lottery, and you never know what tomorrow will hold, like a chocolate bar that is bitter or delicious. It's important to understand that there might be more delicious chocolates every day, regardless of who you are or how satisfied you are with your life. I encourage you to read everything said here from beginning to end. It will make you see the world in a whole new light. After reading the book cover to cover, suppose you've ever desired to be in charge of your own life but weren't quite sure how to achieve it. In that case, you will have the information and abilities necessary to design your reality and achieve much more.

The reason I am telling you this.

You may be asking yourself why I am the one who will show you this amazing route that will turn your journey from a mindless pursuit of dream illusions into a delightful stroll. Dreams are usually mirages that disappear the closer you reach them; they rarely lead anywhere. Transforming dreams into desires may appear like a superficial wordplay, but it hides something deeper. I've always believed that life offers more to me than what my useless, worthless aspirations can provide. Life began to throw me a curveball of hardships and big emotional swings. Dreams don't matter when you're about to mistrust yourself. Everyone has a predetermined fate.

When you learn to see the world through the lens of your spirit, you will start to see it. I spent years trying to figure out what my life's purpose was. I saw that the route is about finding it over time. I started studying life's mysteries and developed a whole new perspective on everything that appeared to have been previously disclosed to us. I started asking questions and looking for answers daily. I was imprisoned in a delusion for half my life, one I would never be able to escape. A person unaware of the power of their existence is like a rickety raft drifting aimlessly on the ocean. It sinks in the first stormy sea that appears. Unaware of the events in our lives or the reasons behind them, we are prone to sinking into a negative mental spiral. A mind without direction will never get very far or reach its full potential. I unintentionally committed a big chunk of my life to becoming a pilot every single day. A developing sense of comprehension and relief eventually surfaced from an emotional ache I didn't comprehend. I realized that I had been viewing everything incorrectly. I was led step by step by destiny to the realization that, as a living creature, I am entitled to the best that life has to offer in the human form. I realized that everything my mind had shown me was completely possible, and everything I had been feeling deep down for a long time made sense. I know now, and it's time for you to understand that every internal urge has a purpose. You are the one who needs to fulfill it. I'll try laying out the steps necessary to fulfill your goals.

What you ought to be able to accomplish following a thorough reading of each chapter.

After reading each chapter from cover to cover, you might want to go back and read them again, focusing even more intently on your improved and new life. Chapter by chapter, you can apply all you learn to your life right now. For you, stepping out from the darkness and out of the never-ending dead end will become a usual formality. Things that were once challenging will eventually become possibilities you were unaware of. You'll come to see everything that has happened in the past as an important lesson, and you'll become someone that people want to take a cue from. I may not agree with the statement that there are as many characters as there are people, but it is a common one. Given the large number of people and the frequent errors in judgment, this remark is more appropriate for those continuously deluded by a false sense of communal awareness. We have become less sensitive because we think someone is better than us. This is now the primary justification for restricting human potential. We are now visitors in our own house. It's time to learn how to carefully manage every emotion that comes your way. It is time for reason to lead you, with the strength of your heart's perception providing unwavering support. You will take on the roles of oppressor and victim, judge and executioner, all in one form because that is who you are. This will educate you to view situations in life from all angles. You'll cease misjudging the actuality you come across. You'll understand that there is just now and that this "now" is your entire reality. There is no past or future. Your past served as a lesson, and you won't be able to create the future you want unless you learn how to impact your "now." Your aspirations hold equal significance to your thoughts during every moment. Right now is the time to take your first concrete move toward the ideal tomorrow.

How To Modify Your Attitude

You will need to alter your perspective if you genuinely want to succeed. It will be necessary for you to alter your perspective about yourself, the environment, and success. Most of the time, your lack of confidence in your ability to succeed is the only thing preventing you from succeeding.

Every day, take some time to reflect and give your thoughts your whole attention. You don't have to be thinking about your expenses or addressing a problem during this time. You should use it for imaginative thought. You truly need to develop your ability to think clearly. Of course, you think about various subjects throughout the day, but does this truly advance you? Take some time to reflect on the subjects that you find interesting.

Modify your perspective. Change your thinking when you start the self-talk we have all engaged in, the belief that you cannot succeed or solve problems. Remember that you are capable of achieving anything. Remember that you can achieve anything if you divide these big objectives into smaller ones.

Keep your attention on the task and recognize where to direct your efforts. When we attempt to concentrate on what we are doing, we frequently discover our thoughts on what has to get done when we get home, what bills need to be paid this week, or what needs to be bought this weekend at the shop. Develop the ability to concentrate on only one item at a time. Yes, that is incredible, am I right? We are taught that multitasking allows us to do numerous tasks simultaneously, but since you are reading this book, I will presume that this approach hasn't resulted in the results you're after. Focus on your home when you are there. Put work first when you're at work. One task at a time will help you become more productive, increase your success, and lower your stress level.

Allow yourself to interact with a variety of individuals and ideas. It will be necessary for you to acknowledge that you might not know every answer. It's possible that you don't know how to complete tasks most efficiently. Permit yourself to learn from others without feeling like you are failing because you don't know the solution.

Recognize that while ideas are fantastic, success comes from following through. It's fantastic if you have a brilliant thought when you're pondering each day. But keep in mind that a concept is useless unless it is carried out completely.

Dismiss "popular" thought. This is frequently someone else's concept that they have accepted because they don't want to take the time to think it through for themselves. This is not thinking. You, on the other hand, will give yourself some alone time to reflect. You must realize that just because your solutions differ from others does not imply that they are incorrect.

Recognize the worth of your thoughts. By doing this, you will start to educate your mind to think only of worthwhile things. I don't want you to cherish your nasty and harsh opinions about other people. Value the opinions you have and the way you see yourself as a person, and choose to focus only on worthwhile ideas.

It is challenging to alter your thought patterns and much more challenging for you to alter your self-perception. You could, however, be able to do so. You need to alter your perspective since, in actuality, no successful person ever told themselves repeatedly that they were a failure. Remind yourself daily that you are successful and will succeed in all you attempt.

Chapter 2: Dissecting the Knot of Stress

Stress is a ubiquitous element that permeates all aspects of our lives, influencing how we react to obstacles. This chapter takes us on a voyage of discovery as we investigate the complex science underlying stress and how comprehending its workings might enable us to overcome the many obstacles we meet in life.

Keanu Reeves: An Introspective and Caring Journey

Early Years and Unexpected Difficulties

The renowned actor Keanu Reeves praised for his composure and fortitude, started a life path woven with stress-related strands. Reeves wasraised in Toronto, Canada, after being born in Beirut, Lebanon. Her early years were characterized by volatility in her family and personal grief. When Keanu was just three years old, his father left the family, leaving a lasting impression on him that he carried into adulthood.

The Development of Emotional Sturdiness

Reeves's ride with life's turbulent currents was far from over. When his partner, Jennifer Syme, gave birth to their stillborn daughter, Ava Archer Syme-Reeves, in 2001, tragedy struck. Reeves's life had a severe emotional shift as a result of this heartbreaking loss. Rather than giving in to the burden of loss, he turned it into an inspiration for developing emotional fortitude.

Comprehending the Stress Knot

Reeves's path is a tutorial for untangling the intricate web of stress. Throughout his career, he overcame personal and professional obstacles, but his perseverance is demonstrated by his steadfast resolve to face these pressures head-on. Reeves met every obstacle, be it the demands of his public persona or his struggles, with poise and a steadfast dedication to comprehending stress's psychological and behavioral consequences.

Handling Tough Situations

Reeves faced numerous challenges during his career that might have easily derailed his path. He had to endure the arduous film production schedules, unceasing media scrutiny, and the weight of personal tragedy. His resilience in the face of difficulty emphasizes how crucial it is to comprehend the many forms of stress and how they affect behavior and emotions.

A Source of Inspiration

The life narrative of Keanu Reeves offers guidance to individuals who are trying to untangle the knot of stress in their own lives. His journey, replete with hardships, demonstrates that resilience is the capacity to weather adversity with courage and dignity rather than the absence of stress. Reeves reminds us that by being aware of stress's behavioral and emotional effects, we can better prepare ourselves to meet life's obstacles head-on and come out stronger and wiser on the other side.

In summary

The legacy of Keanu Reeves proves the human spirit's ability to persevere through the complex mazes of stress. His narrative encourages us to resolve stress, develop behavioral and emotional fortitude, and overcome adversity to emerge as resilient fighters rather than victims.

The Physiology of Stress: Dissecting the Body's Reaction to Force

Our bodies' complex biology plays a major role in stress, the silent power that molds our lives. It is critical to comprehend the underlying physiological reactions underlying this intricate phenomenon as we embark on this journey into the very core of stress.

There is a physiological reaction to stress. Our bodies automatically respond to perceived threats by getting ready for a fight-or-flight response, which involves either a physical confrontation or a quick retreat. The hypothalamic-pituitary-adrenal (HPA) axis, a key component in the stress response, coordinates this process. Its start triggers reactions that increase blood pressure and heart rate, preparing the body to respond to the approaching threat. Whether it's a professional about to give an important presentation or a student preparing for an important exam, this response frequently takes the shape of performance anxiety, which is the physical manifestation of the body's preparation to face difficulties head-on.

The HPA axis is a vital survival mechanism that the body can activate, but prolonged activation can harm health. Recurrent activation of this stress response has been linked to several health issues, such as lowered immunity and hypertension. For example, a student who pushes herself to the limit by staying late to finish projects or a professional who constantly works too much could suffer these negative consequences. The body's enduring state of preparedness to face perceived dangers might gradually weaken its resistance, creating conditions for long-term healing problems.

When it comes to stress, cortisol is a major influence. Our bodies release cortisol in the stress reaction, an important hormone that can temporarily increase immunity and energy levels, which helps the body prepare for flight or fight. It's the spike in adrenaline right before a major game or the sharp spike in awareness right before danger arrives. On the other hand, persistently elevated cortisol levels over time can cause several problems. Common side effects include weight gain due to cortisol's role in fat storage and concentration issues. Prolonged stress exposure can leave professionals and students struggling to overcome these obstacles.

Comprehending the complex biology underlying stress is essential as we investigate methods to regulate and lessen its effects. It clarifies the reasons behind our bodies' reactions and emphasizes the value of adaptable coping strategies and resilience in adversity. As we learn more about stress, this information becomes an effective tool in overcoming life's complex obstacles.

How Is Eft Tapping Operational?

Understanding a pattern interrupt and an EFT Tapping statement may help you better grasp how EFT Tapping functions.

1. Acceptance: We say, "I totally and completely accept myself," as the final tap remark. We enter the present moment when we accept. Only when we are in the present moment can we recover?

2. Subconsciously addresses today's dysfunctional beliefs: To improve our lives, we must first eradicate dysfunctional beliefs from our subconscious minds. The "instructions" for the subconscious are in the tapping phrases' center.

3. Pattern interrupt: Energy cannot easily flow along the traditional Chinese meridians due to dysfunctional

memories and/or beliefs. By interrupting the cycle, tapping enables our body's inherent Infinite Wisdom to surface and facilitate recovery.

When a client says, "I fear change," using EFT Tapping, they express a fear of change because * This remark validates the client's dysfunctional thinking and calms the body. * We won't be sidetracked while we tap. For our Truth to emerge, the tapping disturbs the flow of energy.

Chapter 9: EFT Tapping's Advantages

An evidence-based self-help technique to enhance our mental, emotional, and physical health is EFT tapping. More than sixty researchers have carried out more than one hundred studies in ten different countries, proving the efficacy and success of EFT Tapping.

It can lessen stress, anxiety, and desire for food. It is beneficial for people with chronic pain, depression, PTSD, and addictions. Tapping can lessen weariness and boost vitality. Studies have indicated that it leads to a notable improvement in sports performance. It can ease joint discomfort and tense muscles. Happiness and joy increased with improved sleep and decreased discomfort!

EFT Tapping is flexible:

Convictions

Feelings

Self-perceptions

Our Narrative

Ideas

Mental jumble

traumatic recollections

Ten Advantages of EFT Tapping Are As follows:

1. Get Rid of Symptomatic Thoughts and Feelings

We must subconsciously erase and/or change our beliefs to completely change our lives. By subtly eradicating negative emotions and ideas, EFT tapping can transform our lives.

The body is meant to be in a healthy, wellbeing, and wellbeing condition. Discomfiture results from blocked energy. Our body is capable of healing itself when we cut a finger. After unhealthy feelings, events, and ideas have been "deleted," our bodies naturally gravitate toward prosperity, happiness, health, and peace.

2. Enhanced Emotional Health

When we eliminate the negative ideas that make us feel afraid, angry, or depressed, we feel better about ourselves and have more hope for the future.

3. Modifications Are Permanent

When an unhealthy, dysfunctional mindset is removed, the body naturally gravitates towards wellbeing. The adjustments we make with EFT are, therefore, irreversible.

4. Lessen Tension and Fear

According to research, tapping can calm the brain's amygdala and dramatically lower levels of the stress hormone cortisol. This promotes calmer feelings and clearer thinking. Reduced stress improves sleep, making one feel less exhausted and more energized. Additionally, there was a decrease in blood pressure and resting heart rate.

5. Emotional Desensitisation

We can tap the sentence, "This difficult person [or their name] ignores and criticizes me," if a difficult person in our lives ignores and/or criticizes us.

Tapping can help us become less sensitive to their behavior, but it doesn't guarantee they won't continue to neglect or criticize us. Our senses and cognitive processes become more refined after we have become emotionally desensitized. Our capacity to make defensible decisions has increased. We avoid taking anything personally. Our wellbeing is not adversely affected. Our faces no longer flush with rage and frustration, our hearts no longer beat 100 beats per minute, and smoke no longer escapes our ears.

6. Reduce Food Cravings and Accelerate Loss of Weight

In 2018, 96 overweight persons participated in a study. Brain scans following four weeks of tapping revealed alterations in the area of the brain linked to cravings. The individuals noted less interest in food. Tapping can aid in weight loss by altering brain regions that trigger food cravings.

Unresolved problems that lie behind the urge to eat are the cause of overeating and emotional eating. Tapping has been shown to help cure the underlying causes surrounding the impulse to overeat, in addition to helping with the physical urge to binge and emotionally eat.

7. Strengthen Your Immune System

White blood cell production has been demonstrated to rise with EFT tapping, which helps strengthen our immune system.

8. Traumas Other Than Post-Traumatic Stress Disorder (PTSD)

Not just veterans of combat experience PTSD. Any number of events can cause trauma and PTSD, including being in an accident of any kind, surviving a natural disaster, school shootings, learning that one has a fatal illness, and being the victim of abuse, including sexual assault.

Much research has been conducted on PTSD. Studies have revealed that EFT Tapping dramatically reduced and/or eliminated individuals' PTSD, as well as their nightmares and flashbacks, sleeplessness, difficulty focusing, feelings of isolation, hypervigilance, and hostility.

According to a 2013 study, after three tapping sessions, 60% of war veterans said their PTSD had subsided. After six tapping sessions, another thirty percent said their PTSD was gone.

Section Six

THE THING THAT IS NEAREST TO A MAGIC PILL

Living a healthy lifestyle alters not just your physical appearance but also your mental state, outlook, and emotional state. Furthermore, physical activity is essential if you want your mind to be at its most creative, optimistic state.

Blood flow to every body region, including the brain, is increased by physical activity, which acts as fuel. Numerous hormones are also released, some of which contribute to the brain's ability to think more clearly.

Even 20 minutes of exercise boosted information processing, according to a recent study from the University of

Georgia's Department of Exercise Science.

Not only that, though. In addition, exercise promotes the development of neurons, which are brain nerve cells that underpin behavioral and cognitive processes.

This means you are not allowing your brain to function to its maximum capacity if you spend all day lounging on your sofa.

Take note of those who sit still for eight hours a day at work. They return home exhausted, tired, and unable to concentrate. One of them used to be me.

When I worked in a corporate setting, two to three hours of nonstop computer use would cause me to feel "numb." At the time, I wasn't going to the gym. It combined to deplete my mental stamina, so I was unwilling to engage in conversation. It was really difficult to be joyful and excited about anything at all.

The only thing you would have gotten in return for asking me to produce any creative work would have been a "blank stare." I could not handle complicated activities and be enthusiastic or creative in any way.

Nope. That was all impossible.

Finally, after experiencing "mind numbness" for months, I decided to take action. I started reading about the connection between physical movement and brain health.

I made a modest beginning.

I started getting up from my chair at my workplace every 30 minutes and performing 20 minutes of light running in the morning. I essentially increased the amount of "movement" in my everyday life.

The outcomes exceeded my expectations. I began to feel better. My enthusiasm and attitude lifted, as did my energy levels. My vitality and involvement increased. My abrupt change in demeanor astonished everyone in my office. All began to value this new ' me.' People began praising me a lot (presumably encouraging me to continue this way).

If I had merely walked around more, I would never have guessed that I would have so much great energy. It was very startling, to be honest. Although I had read that exercise depletes energy rather than replenishes it, it's incredibly effective to EXPERIENCE it.

I have continued to live this way ever since. I now walk thirty minutes and meditate fifteen minutes in the morning. I get physical and mental vigor from it that lasts all day.

I strongly advise engaging in physical activity for at least thirty minutes daily. You can exercise with weights, cardio, yoga, tai chi, jogging, walking, or cycling. Please talk with your physician before beginning.

Apart from the morning routine, stand up from your chair every 30 minutes to extend your limbs. Go for a quick stroll around the workplace. Proceed to the water cooler, fill up your glass and return. Simply get up and take a little stroll.

For ten days, attempt to do both of these. Your optimism and energy levels would significantly increase. It gives your day more 'life' and revitalizes your body and mind.

It also makes perfect sense considering this lifestyle's long-term health advantages.

Make Use Of Your Strong Mind

Isn't it remarkable that we have conscious minds that allow us to focus on anything we want at any given time and that we are in charge of our lives? Isn't it fantastic that we also possess a subconscious mind that controls our bodies, maintains our hearts, heals our bodies, and provides us with the incredible ability to manifest our desires?

A thorough investigation of the mind's true potential reveals that just 4 percent of its capacity is aware, with the remaining 96% being subconscious. Thus, by understanding this, we must know how crucial it is to use our subconscious minds. Whether we are driving and go off into a trance, and when we wake up, we realize we were thinking about everything we needed to get done, or we are going to bed and dreaming.

Have you carried out the task before? When you wake up thirty minutes after daydreaming while driving a car, you ask yourself, "Who has been driving this car? I can't remember the trip?" When you have done something so frequently that you no longer need to be aware of it, you are in what is known as a trance. It's similar to your first driving experience when you knew it was unfamiliar and uncomfortable.

However, after a few tries and you get the hang of it, you can do it instinctively, and if you have a license, you never get anxious about driving since you have thousands of driving experiences under your belt. Your mind is everything; it has the power to propel you to great heights and, conversely, to just keep you safe, which will ultimately prevent you from leading a life you can be proud of. All personal changes must be made at the subconscious level for them to take hold. If they do, you will have changed who you are entirely from what you would have been had you only made the conscious changes.

How many people do you know that consciously decide to change and try to follow a diet, but how long does that change last? It doesn't last because they are forcing themselves to do it, and change won't come about right away until your two minds cooperate.

As a life coach, I encounter many issues that people face daily. I've found that these individuals often have ingrained patterns from their early years that they didn't realize were there. Whether it's an instinctive behavior you've trained yourself to do or a limiting belief—one of the strongest emotions a person may experience—once things are brought to light, the person can alter them.

As a coach, I look for ways to help clients uncover their self-limiting beliefs and implement strategies to help them overcome them, regardless of whether they think they can or cannot. A belief is a conviction about something's meaning; altering your beliefs will improve everything in your life.

The five senses—visual (see), auditory (hear), kinaesthetic (feel), olfactory (smell), and gustatory (taste)—are how we perceive the outside world. Without you realizing it, this is also occurring automatically and subconsciously. Your unconscious mind is working nonstop to heal and find a solution if you have an injury, sore throat, illness, or strained muscle. Our unconscious mind never shuts off when we are asleep, which is why many people listen to successful CDs before bed to continue learning unknowingly.

Have you ever had dreams that defy logic? If so, this is likely the result of your unconscious mind operating automatically. Every memory you have ever had is also stored in your subconscious mind. Because the unconscious mind and the body have such a close link, the unconscious mind is hardwired to always seek out more.

They collaborate to provide you with the greatest experience and ensure your survival. Additionally, it takes everything personally, so everything you say about another person makes your unconscious mind believe you are saying the same thing about yourself. This is because the unconscious mind is a different kind of force; it does not distinguish between me and you but views us as one. We are distinct from one another in situations where the conscious mind acts as a dividing force. This is particularly intriguing when it comes to dreams, as you may occasionally experience being someone else or seeing someone else perform an action you would typically perform.

Since everything is taken personally, if you start saying negative things about others, your subconscious will likely believe you are bad. You will probably notice this with people you know who make fun of other people; you should avoid associating with them since they have turned into negative people. However, you will perceive yourself as such if you find everything about other people to be wonderful and spectacular and you adore their actions. Additionally, our unconscious mind's goal is simply to keep us alive and make life as easy as possible, so venturing outside our comfort zone can sometimes be exhilarating and terrifying. Because your mind must adjust to what you are asking, retraining our thoughts by stepping outside our comfort zones will become easier and easier with time.

Chapter 3: Step #2: Apply Your Capabilities to Solve Problems Effectively

Analytical abilities and efficient problem-solving lead to wise decisions. You won't overcome obstacles without comprehending and solving a problem. Here are a few practical and effective methods to discover that:

Discover How To Identify The Correct Problem

Frequently, we become entangled in massive issues one after another—not because we cannot handle them, but because we cannot pinpoint their underlying causes.

Unable to solve the correct problem typically leads to further mayhem and stuckness. Before it's too late, find out the true problem to help alleviate this one. Here are some guidelines to make sure that:

• Attempt to pay attention to the various facets of your existence. Daily attention to your relationships, health, finances, and other areas will help you recognize the early warning signals of developing issues. For example, failing to pay a bill on time indicates that you have a problem with your money management and should take immediate action to prevent the situation from worsening. When you identify some problems, note them and consider both the short- and long-term effects. This aids in your comprehension of the nature of the issue and the dangers it is expected to present.

•Pay attention to the source of the issue and, if necessary, seek professional assistance. To identify the cause of the problem, thoroughly investigate every other associated factor. If you see a problem with your company's sales, it might not result from your sales department's shortcomings but rather a problem with the advertising strategy.

If you keep thinking that your health is failing due to a regular cold, you could never get checked out and discover that you have a digestive system issue. Only once you've identified the true issue can you come up with the best plan of action to address it. Prioritise addressing the true nature of the issue before it's too late.

Develop a solution-focused mindset.

Once the issue has been located, comprehend it and concentrate on resolving it. Of course, concentrating on the issue is also crucial. Still, if you continue to analyze it in isolation, you'll just grow more anxious and unable to take any significant steps to address it. Rather, concentrate on identifying the appropriate remedy.

Every time you find yourself in a rut, ask yourself questions like "How can I resolve it?" and "What can be done to fix it now?" or "How can things be improved?" Research indicates that your brain is programmed to respond precisely to your questions. Asking yourself, "Why does it happen to me?" can only lead to responses demonstrating how deserving you are of your current predicament. Having said that, if you brainstorm solutions for the problem, you'll quickly run out of ideas for how to solve it.

Bom Kim founded the South Korean internet retailer Coupang in 2010, and as of right now, they bring in $4 billion in revenue annually. One of their concerns was getting goods delivered effectively in a nation with a dense population. They were limited to using the truck size permitted by the city for delivery because 528 people live in each square kilometer in the nation. The vehicles had to make multiple daily trips from the nearby warehouse to the customer's home, creating two major problems: delivery delays and delivery costs. They decided to give their truck and package appearance a major makeover. The Coupang team identified the issue and took significant action to fix it promptly, according to a quote from Bom Kim. Remember that whenever you encounter an issue, concentrate on finding answers rather than criticizing yourself or wondering why it happened to you.

Consider Why.

Asking oneself "why" and "what caused it" at every turn is a terrific method to get to the bottom of an issue, which is essential to finding an appropriate solution. When faced with an issue, ask yourself, "Why does it exist?" and keep asking questions until you find the answer.

If you're having trouble understanding why your money is being mismanaged, ask yourself why. If the response is that you were not paid in full, return your attention to the "why." If you determine this occurred due to your ten-day absence from work, consider why again. Continue doing so until you identify the underlying problem; then, develop solutions. Consider the benefits and drawbacks of each recommendation before choosing the one that carries the fewest risks.

Utilize the "What If" Approach.

The "what if" method will help your brain develop novel solutions to your challenges and stimulate creative thought. Consider questions like "What if I try this?" and "How about I go this way?" After you've completed that, record the responses in writing. This strategy often helps you think more clearly and generates creative and intriguing thoughts.

Seek Assistance: Frequently, we are too arrogant to request assistance, thinking that doing so would prove our incapacity. This is untrue since everyone needs direction and assistance occasionally, and asking for it is a sign of humanity. Seek assistance from a field specialist if you believe a situation is too difficult for you to handle on your own. Seek advice from a relationship counselor if you are experiencing problems. Contact your uncle- a prosperous serial entrepreneur- if you're worried about your company's declining sales.

Making wise selections just gets easier if you become proficient at addressing problems. More techniques to improve this stage are covered in the following chapter.

Rewriting The Script: How To Rewire Your Thought Process

The advantages of cognitive reframing are discussed in this chapter. You'll comprehend the detrimental mental misconceptions people frequently encounter and how they appear. Additionally, you will discover what neuroplasticity is, how to enhance it, and how it might assist you in restructuring your mental processes. Lastly, five easy yet powerful techniques will help you change your thoughts.

Reframe Thinking Cognitively

Your thoughts shape your perception of the world and have a

powerful influence on your actions. Thought patterns frequently originate from people's beliefs, which is why they cause unhealthful feelings and behaviors. For example, you may constantly worry about losing your job or getting bad reviews if your skill level needs to be improved. This may result in negative feelings like tension and irritation, as well as anxiety and other mental health conditions. This makes it more difficult for you to focus and give your best work at work, which feeds into your sense of inadequacy.

The technique of rephrasing your ideas to alter how you view particular events and circumstances is known as cognitive reframing. It necessitates changing your negative thought habits to more constructive and optimistic ones. Your mental and emotional well-being will improve because of this; if you practice it consistently, your new ideas will eventually become your default way of thinking.

During this procedure, you must practice self-awareness and pay attention to your mental patterns. In this manner, you can identify negative ideas as soon as they arise and take action before it's too late. Negative ideas will have a greater influence and power over your perceptions, moods, behaviors, and sentiments the longer you let them fester in your mind.

You can also use cognitive reframing to change how you react to stress. Elevated cortisol levels and the start of the body's fight-or-flight response are linked to stress. The stress reaction will be triggered by any circumstance you consider somewhat dangerous. Your body will react to high amounts of stress by raising your heart rate, making you sweat, breathing more deeply, or giving you chills, for example.

You can manage your stress and reduce your stress reaction by learning how to think differently. This method promotes relaxation and helps you see the situation from several angles.

Understanding the kind of cognitive distortion you're dealing with will help you confront your negative ideas more effectively. Irrational thought patterns, known as cognitive distortions, can have startling consequences on your general well-being. Many people encounter several cognitive illusions daily. However, a strong propensity towards these thought patterns can result in undesired behaviors and persistently bad feelings. Knowing the many types of cognitive illnesses enables you to identify them when they occur and replace them with more constructive ideas.

Some of the most typical cognitive distortions that people encounter are as follows:

Think Everything or Nothing

The propensity to see just two possible outcomes in any given circumstance is a characteristic of this cognitive distortion. All-or-nothing thinkers believe that everything will work out perfectly and go their way, or everything will go wrong, and the worst-case scenario will pass.

Very few things in life can be categorized as having a wholly positive or successful consequence or a wholly negative or unsuccessful outcome. Most situations fall on a spectrum, with different aspects influencing their results and how people view them. All-or-nothing thinkers frequently overlook these subtleties and exhibit excessive thought patterns when the best-case scenario doesn't materialize. For example, athletes may believe they would never amount to anything in their sports career if they performed worse than expected in a single competition.

Reading Minds

This kind of cognitive distortion is especially common among those who have social anxiety. Making assumptions and attempting to infer what other people think is known as mind-reading. These presumptions are typically unfavorable and supported by scant to no evidence. This way of thinking makes people aware of even the smallest verbal or nonverbal clues. It interprets them as indicating that the other person is bored, irritated, or frustrated with them.

Someone suffering from this cognitive distortion might interpret a friend looking at their watch, for instance, as an indication that they're bored and ready to go. There are, perhaps, further explanations. They might just be checking the clock; they might have an appointment or something crucial to undertake in the coming hours.

Oversimplification

The tendency to assume that a situation's rules apply to all similar ones is known as overgeneralization. You can be discouraged from pursuing new experiences and opportunities because you believe they would all result in the same things. This will hinder your personal development and impact your social and professional life. Overgeneralizers may shy away from meeting new people due to a negative dating experience. They'll think they're not very adept at dating or never find someone.

Mental Screening

"mental filtering" describes how someone focuses on particular elements of a circumstance. Individuals with this cognitive distortion typically focus on the negative features of any given scenario while ignoring its positive qualities. They get a romantic view of the world and believe that nothing is biased against them, which breeds ungraciousness and a pessimistic outlook. For instance, students can believe they are failing their classes if they obtain one low grade. The numerous occasions in which they received excellent grades on examinations and assignments, the outstanding projects they completed, and the quantity of effort they put into their studies will all be disregarded.

Through cognitive reframing, these distortions can be disproved and broken down. You must recognize negative thought patterns, confront them, consider the reasons behind your irrational thoughts and beliefs, and reframe them into more sensible and constructive ones.

You can work on rephrasing your thoughts on your own. However, it can be a drawn-out process that demands a lot of concentration, willpower, and concentration. Consulting a mental health expert can be quite beneficial, particularly if you frequently battle with negative ideas. Specifically intended to assist people in identifying and replacing harmful thought patterns with more constructive and beneficial ones.Depression, substance misuse, marital issues, anxiety disorders. Distortions in cognition and other problematic thought processes are the root cause of most of these diseases, or they aggravate them.

Let's say you want to begin cognitive reframing by yourself. If so, you need to know how cognitive distortions impact how you perceive the outside world. Several mindfulness practices, like body scans and mindful journaling, let you identify unwelcome thoughts as they come up. You have more time to consider your ideas and give yourself time to doubt their practicality before acting on them when you put your thoughts down in writing. By journaling and body scanning, you can learn to distinguish between intrusive ideas and your genuine, original thoughts.

Chapter 5: Adapting Your Thoughts

Strong beliefs influence our decisions and behaviors in life. People occasionally harbor limiting thoughts that may prevent them from achieving their goals and being happy. Stress, anxiety, and reluctance to attempt new things can be triggered by restricting or negative ideas. These ideas, influenced by upbringing, culture, society, and prior experiences, are frequently automatic and subconscious. It's crucial to alter your views if you want to do big things in life.

Though it can be difficult, changing your views is not insurmountable. Here are some tried-

and-true methods for working on your belief modification:

1. Recognise Adverse Beliefs

The first step is finding your limiting beliefs that prevent you from moving forward. Analyze your thought processes and identify the beliefs preventing you from realizing your goals. Put these ideas in writing and consider their detrimental effects on your life.

For example, if you think you're not smart enough, you probably won't apply for jobs requiring intellectual skills or take chances. This mindset will keep you from seizing fresh chances and challenges that can improve your life.

2. Examine Your Thoughts

The next stage is confronting your limiting ideas once you've identified them. Consider whether facts support your opinions or if they are justifiable. By challenging some of your beliefs, you might become aware that they are unfounded and false.

You can replace harmful beliefs with constructive and empowering ones when you question your existing ones. Consider what you would do if your limiting beliefs were gone. This will inspire you to form new beliefs that support your aspirations and aims.

3. Be in the company of positive influences

You can alter your beliefs by surrounding yourself with positive influences. Taking on the mindset of others who share your positive outlook is simpler. These people can provide you with encouragement, support, and fresh insights.

Look for a coach or mentor to motivate you to alter your beliefs. Review publications or articles offering insightful advice on altering one's beliefs. Consider involvement with a community or group that promotes growth and personal development.

4. Illustration

One powerful method that can assist you in altering your beliefs is visualization. Imagine what your life would be like if such restrictive ideas didn't exist. Use your imagination to visualize the kind of person you want to be and the kind of life you want.

Using visualization, you may rewire your subconscious mind and weaken the influence of unfavorable thoughts. Frequent visualization can strengthen your new beliefs and have a beneficial effect.

5. Act

And lastly, altering your views requires action. You can reinforce your new views by taking consistent activity that aligns with them. Take baby steps first and work your way up to reach your goals.

For instance, if you think you're not talented enough to write a book, begin by penning short pieces or blogs. You will get more self-assured and confident with time, and you can write a book one day.

Though it takes time and work, changing one's ideas is worthwhile. Adopting new beliefs can enhance your life and bring happiness and fulfillment. Remember to be persistent and patient as you work to alter your views.

Bringing Your Inner Drive To Life

Finding Your Unique Motivations

It might be simple to lose sight of our objectives and give in to the temptation of giving up when faced with difficulty and adversity. But at these trying times, we have to go down deep and find the will to persevere. Recognizing our true motivations to ignite our inner fire and build the resilience required to conquer any challenge is crucial.

Being motivated is a unique and personal experience. What motivates and inspires one individual could not have the same impact on another. To realize your greatest potential for achievement, you must recognize your unique sources of motivation.

Reflecting on yourself is the first step towards determining what motivates you personally. Consider for a moment what genuinely energizes and makes you happy. What pursuits or objectives give you a sense of excitement and life? These can be effective motivators and are frequently signs of your hobbies. Understanding your passions is essential to finding long-lasting motivation for career success, a creative endeavor, or volunteer work for a cause close to your heart.

Your basic values are an additional crucial factor to take into account. Which values are important to you and drive your choices? Knowing your values will enable you to match your objectives with your priorities. For instance, if you are a family person, you can be driven by the desire to give your loved ones a better life. You may develop a strong feeling of purpose that will propel you forward even in the face of difficulty by aligning your goals with your values.

Furthermore, looking back at your successes and accomplishments might provide insightful information about your motivations. Remember the moments when you felt most successful and proud of yourself. What elements played a part in those achievements? Was it the sense of having made a difference, the acknowledgment you got, or the development you went through as a person? You can find trends and motivators that you can use to tackle new difficulties by examining these instances.

Recall that there is no one-size-fits-all definition of motivation. It is particular to every person. As you move through difficult situations, give yourself time to reflect and figure out what inspires you to keep going. You can access a source of inspiration that will help you succeed in all facets of your life by knowing your values, passions, and past achievements.

The book Fueling the Fire Within Discovering Motivation for Success aims to inspire those going through difficult times to never give up. To assist readers in discovering their motivators and developing the will to succeed in life and overcome obstacles, it provides useful tools and ideas. Through personal motivation, readers will acquire the resilience and tenacity required to surmount hurdles in life and accomplish their objectives.

Embracing Your Purpose and Passion

It's natural to feel like giving up and lose enthusiasm when faced with difficult circumstances. But it's precisely in these trying times that discovering your purpose and passion becomes the more important. We will look at how to find the inner fire within you and find the drive to get past whatever challenges life presents in this chapter.

Achieving success in life begins with discovering your passion. The motivation keeps you going forward even when it seems like the deck is stacked against you. Think for a moment about what genuinely excites you. Which pursuits or causes make you happy and fulfilled? What draws you in naturally?

Matching your passion with your purpose after you've found it is critical. Our acts take on significance and direction when a purpose guides them. Consider the question, "How can I use my passion to make a difference in the world?" Knowing your mission can help you stay motivated and give you the willpower to overcome obstacles and hardships.

It's crucial to have a resilient mindset and never give up if you want to discover your passion and purpose. While failures and setbacks are inevitable, they do not define you. Rather, see these times as chances for development and education. Be in the company of positive people and take inspiration from individuals who have conquered comparable obstacles. Make connections with people who share your aims and desires. Their encouragement and support will motivate you to keep going when things get hard.

Furthermore, see yourself succeeding and keep returning to the reason you began this trip in the first place. Make a vision board or maintain a journal to track your development and recognize your accomplishments as you go. You can maintain your motivation and never lose sight of what counts if you constantly remind yourself of your passion and purpose.

In conclusion, one of life's most effective strategies for overcoming obstacles and misfortune is connecting with your passion and purpose. By discovering your true motivation, integrating it with your mission, and developing a resilient attitude, you may kindle the inner fire within yourself and find the drive required to succeed. Never forget that you can persevere through difficult circumstances and design a life that fulfills you and has meaning.

Chapter 3: Putting Positive in Place of Negative

Starting on the path to happiness is as simple as recognizing bad thoughts with awareness. Many of us engage in complaining talks or just mentally recite unfavorable words.

Whenever you had a negative thought, said something terrible, or participated in a negative conversation, you could fill a notebook in a single day if you kept track of it.

One approach to taking charge of your happiness is recognizing unpleasant thoughts when they arise. Every time a negative thought crosses your mind, change it by giving it a positive spin or acting constructively.

With further practice, your skills in this area will improve significantly. The objective is to identify and transform as many negative beliefs as possible.

Your subconscious receives a signal whenever you swap out bad thinking for constructive behavior or concepts.

Your subconscious will concentrate on the positive thoughts more quickly the more you do this.

Between your conscious and autonomic nerve systems, you are creating a bridge.

How to Put an End to a Negative Idea

Say "stop" to yourself as soon as the notion comes. When a negative idea arises, interrupt it using "stop." This will assist you in becoming consumed by it.

When a bad notion arises, explain why you think it and provide evidence. What initially caused the notion to occur?

Get a journal and put your negative thoughts down in writing. Go through your journal and explain the ideas and actions. Dismantle your preconceived notions and record any fresh insights you have gained.

The ideal outcome is to replace a negative thought before it manifests into negative behavior. A bad thought can lead to a negative action. For example, you might tell yourself, "I hate speaking in front of crowds. I am so awkward," when you know you have to talk in front of your colleagues tomorrow.

It's untrue to tell yourself that you find public speaking uncomfortable due to your awkwardness.

Even though you may feel uncomfortable, you are not; if you were, you wouldn't be required to speak in front of a large group of people for work.

Tell the truth and come up with a different idea. For example, "I feel uncomfortable speaking in front of groups of people," is not as depressing as the initial one.

The more skillfully you identify and intercept those negative thoughts, the more proficient you will be in substituting good, uplifting remarks and thoughts for those negative ones.

When you have time, review the negative sentiments you wrote down and revise them to be more genuine and accurate.

You'll be pleasantly pleased at how fast this exercise alters the way you think.

It seems that the easiest method to decompress is to let off steam when we're anxious. You are simply making things worse if you use your complaints and exaggerations as a way to vent. The best "blow off steam" method is engaging in a positive, enjoyable activity.

By doing something you enjoy, you can replace the negative thoughts and feelings from the day with pleasant ones.

It won't make you feel better to whine about the awful things that happened during the day; instead, doing something you enjoy will turn the bad into a positive. Finish your day with a smile.

Happiness is mostly dependent on having a positive self-image and using positive affirmations. It's true what they say: "If you don't love yourself, you can't love someone else."

Positive feelings that unite people are harder to access if you have low self-esteem. Positive affirmations will only take you so far; happiness requires both.

Uplifting and encouraging comments are known as positive affirmations.

Respecting and loving oneself is necessary to develop and preserve a positive self-image. Jot down five of your best traits, then tell yourself what you wrote. When you feel low about yourself, remember these five attributes and use them.

Searching the internet for positive affirmations is the simplest approach to locating them. Spend some time looking up positive affirmations and quotes online; millions are accessible. Once you've found your favorites, jot them down and store them in your diary.

Using these affirmations, you can communicate your feelings about yourself.

Spend a few minutes reading through your positive affirmations if stress gets to you or you are having a rough day. They will support you in overcoming negativity. When things don't go according to plan, never be too hard on yourself or punish yourself. Recall that you are not the adversary; you only want what's best for yourself.

You have less time to be aware of negativity. The more of your attention is directed towards happy thoughts and emotions.

Putting Your Attention On Positivity

Think about an empty glass sitting next to a water jug on a table. After filling the glass halfway, you pour water into it. In your opinion, is the glass half full or half empty? With this time-tested test, you may find out if you are an optimist or a pessimist. If you perceive the glass as half full, you are an optimist with a positive mindset; however, if you see it as half empty, you are pessimistic and have a negative attitude toward life. Straightforward but effective.

To ensure you can take advantage of the positivity surrounding you, practicing positive thinking means being an optimist and seeking out the positive aspects of life to concentrate on. It feels amazing to be upbeat. Being happy all the time is challenging, though, because life is full of possibilities to encounter negativity. As a result, thinking positively demands deliberate effort on your part.

A Negative Day

Imagine having a wonderful mood when you get up in the morning. The sun is shining, you're on time, and everything is going well. You switch on the radio to learn about the current traffic state and hear a breaking news report about a serious vehicle crash involving fifteen people. You suddenly don't feel as upbeat. You get to work on schedule, and just as you feel better about yourself, you get summoned into your boss's office. A client has expressed dissatisfaction with your work and requested a redo. Your optimistic disposition declines once again as you start to question your skills.

As you battle to repeat the client's work, you discover that you get easily irritated with your coworkers and that your negative attitude causes them to avoid you or react negatively to you. The wonderful day that began has now entirely given way to negativity.

The intriguing thing about the whole situation is that by concentrating on good thoughts, you can alter every unpleasant event. The issue was that you were not actively thinking positive thoughts to make sure that the negative thoughts did not have a chance to take root, even though it may not have seemed like you were actively thinking bad thoughts or drawing negativity.

This is how things may have turned out differently for you. It was inappropriate for you to turn on the radio in the morning to listen to the traffic updates. Rather, you ought to have adopted an optimistic outlook and anticipated smooth traffic when traveling to your place of employment. When you were summoned to your boss's office at work, you should have accepted that you might not be in agreement and sought out the specific issue so that you could address it rather than letting the client's comments damage your self-worth. Your coworkers can drastically change your workplace environment if you can always be upbeat and kind, regardless of the challenges you may be facing. Good vibes always come back to you.

One must adopt an optimistic outlook on circumstances to make an impression amidst the masses of negativity. One of the keys to thinking positively is this.

What Makes Positivity Vital?

You can always live a more fulfilling life than the one you lead. Consider it. You must feel that there is anything in your life that can be changed or improved upon to bring you happiness and contentment. Thinking positively is the simplest approach to carrying out such transformation. Being able to create affirmations, occupy one's mind with constructive ideas, maintain optimism, and silence one's negative inner voice are all characteristics of positive thinking. You will learn how to cultivate positivity in the upcoming chapter.

www.ingramcontent.com/pod-product-compliance
Lightning Source LLC
Chambersburg PA
CBHW052138110526
44591CB00012B/1775